"To win in the marketplace you must first win in the workplace."

— *DOUG CONANT*, CEO OF CAMPBELL'S SOUP

"When people are financially invested, they want a return. When people are emotionally invested, they want to contribute."

— *SIMON SINEK*, BESTSELLING AUTHOR OF *"START WITH WHY"*

"Always treat your employees exactly as you want them to treat your best customers."

— *STEPHEN R. COVEY*, BESTSELLING AUTHOR OF *"THE 7 HABITS OF HIGHLY EFFECTIVE PEOPLE"*

"Appreciate everything your associates do for the business. Nothing else can quite substitute for a few well-chosen, well-timed, sincere words of praise. They're absolutely free and worth a fortune."

— *SAM WALTON*, FOUNDER OF *"WAL-MART"*

"I consider my ability to arouse enthusiasm among men the greatest asset I possess. The way to develop the best that is in a man is by appreciation and encouragement."

— *CHARLES SCHWAB*, FOUNDER OF *CHARLES SCHWAB CORPORATION*

"The only way to do great work is to love what you do."

— *STEVE JOBS*, FOUNDER OF *APPLE*

All rights reserved. Copyright © 2020 by Anita Emoff

7 Deadly Myths: That Will Destroy Company Culture, Workforce Engagement, & Sales Growth

KING OF KINGS

King of Kings Publishing
12837 Louetta Road, Suite 203
Cypress, TX 77429
www.kingofkingspublishing.com
@kingofkingspublishing

No part of this book may be reproduced in any form or by any electronic or mechanical means, including information storage and retrieval systems, without written permission from the author, except for the use of brief quotations in a book review.

The 7 myths shared in this book come from data, case studies, and proven results and experience during Boost Engagement's lifetime as an expert in workforce engagement and sales since the early 1950s.

What you'll learn in this book is not opinions, hearsay, or conjecture, but backed up by multiple publications, reports, and studies to educate Human Resources departments, managers, supervisors, and leaders in small, medium, and large businesses, companies, and organizations in how to engage their employees effectively and grow in their niches and industries rapidly no matter the environment.

Our hope is that you'll use what you discover in the following pages to empower your workforce with new, innovative incentives and rewards to boost their engagement, their excitement to work for you, and increase your sales and their buy-in to your organization.

Give us a call or send us an email. We'd love to help.

info@cogzvault.com | 800-466-2705

For all of the Human Resources experts out there who want a powerful employee experience...

7 DEADLY MYTHS

THAT WILL DESTROY YOUR COMPANY CULTURE, WORKFORCE ENGAGEMENT, & SALES GROWTH

ANITA EMOFF
Chairman of Boost Engagement

YOU'VE BEEN DUPED!

As a business manager or the head of a small- to medium-sized organization, you want to get the most out of your team.

Some managers focus on discipline: creating strict guidelines for employees to follow so that they can avoid time-wasting activities and be as productive as possible.

Other managers try to keep things fun and loose: believing that a positive environment is the main key to success.

And while there are kernels of truth to both approaches, they overlook one simple fact.

The most productive workers are the most *engaged*.

And that engagement leads to success for the entire company.

Don't believe it? "Only 42% of U.S. employees look forward to coming to work, compared to 84% at Fortune 100 Best Companies to Work For."[1]

How do managers engage their employees?
With emotional loyalty to their company.
Too many small to medium sized business owners and managers buy into self-limiting myths that are not just harming morale, but severely impacting the bottom line.
These 7 myths are dangerous.
But the good news is, they are rather easy to overcome.
Before you overcome them, you need to know what they are...

1

MYTH #1
JUST GIVE THEM A RAISE!

When anyone thinks of making employees happy, the first thing that comes to mind is the paycheck.

It makes sense, too: when applying for a job, the first consideration is usually how much money you're going to make.

We're all here to get paid, right?

So it would stand to reason that increasing engagement among your staff just means adding a few dollars to their paychecks.

It follows a pretty straightforward line of logic.

Everyone is happy when they get a raise!

When a manager is competing with another company for a potential employee, the first offer is higher pay.

"What are they paying you? I'll pay more!"

And think of the stereotypical job interview on TV or in movies, where it seems the only thing anyone wants to talk about is the paycheck (including the ever-realistic move of writing down the salary number on a piece of paper and sliding it across the desk - who does that?).

THERE'S NO PROOF FOR THIS CLICHE.

Before we get into reasons why this idea is incorrect, let's be clear about something: there are no studies that suggest more money is the path to higher employee engagement and/or retention.

Human behavioral expert Alfie Kohn summed it up nicely[1]: "No controlled scientific study has ever found a long-term enhancement of the quality of work as a result of any financial reward system."

When you are trying to make big decisions for your company, you want them to be rooted in facts and data.

There is no shortage of data on workers, productivity, and morale in the workplace.

But despite the thousands of hours that have been analyzed in offices all over the world, there just isn't any evidence to support the idea that you just need to give everybody a raise.

THIS IS GOOD NEWS!

At first, you might be annoyed by this.

After all, it's the easiest solution possible, isn't it?

Throwing a few dollars at an unhappy employee is an efficient way to boost morale.

But it's also an expensive one.

If you have a team of 10 employees and they are all unhappy, giving them a $100/month raise would cost you $12,000/year.

Maybe that's worth it, but you would likely have to shuffle around your company finances to absorb that kind of expense.

So it's good that greater pay isn't that effective at increasing employee engagement.

It means you have options.

You might actually be surprised at how many...

THERE ARE PLENTY OF WAYS TO ADDRESS CONCERNS BEFORE YOU LOOK AT PAY.

There have been several studies conducted[2] that shed some light on where higher pay sits on the priorities of the average worker.

In one, employees ranked a desire for higher pay as *ninth* on the list of reasons why they were leaving their current place of employment.

Ninth!

Who would have guessed that it would fall that far down the list?

Another study showed that only 20% of employees labeled "salary" as their highest contributor to company loyalty.

That means you could offer raises to 80% of employees and they would still be unhappy and willing to leave their jobs.

WHAT DOES THIS REALLY MEAN?

This could be confusing on the surface.

It defies the commonly-accepted narrative that money is the prime motivator for workers.

Let's start with what it doesn't mean: this information does not mean we can't demonstrate our appreciation for our employees with financial incentives and raises.

These things are appreciated, and they need to be done.

You can't build a healthy company culture and still underpay your employees.

That can't happen.

But it can't be the *only* thing.

When you throw money at an employee, you are engaging in a strategy that offers diminishing returns over time.

That's because the money you spend on an employee becomes the new normal.

A raise is great - at first. After a few months, however, everyone adjusts to it.

And if the morale is still low, then you'd have to offer additional raises and bonuses to the employee to keep that morale high.

The snowball effect kicks in, and suddenly you find yourself spending far too much money on someone - no matter who the employee is.

In 2003, T.A. Atchison summed it up this way[3]: "As soon as money is predictable, it becomes an entitlement, not a motivator."

Let's go a little deeper.

SATISFIED VS. ENGAGED

Money is an incredibly useful tool for employers.

But it is, at the end of the day, the basis of a transaction.

When you are paying your employees what they are worth, they feel satisfied with that arrangement.

That's what you want... to a point.

But is a satisfied employee an *engaged* employee?

No.

Just because a worker is happy doesn't mean they are engaged with the process of doing the work.

It just means they're happy.

They're satisfied when they open their paychecks.

There's a difference between that and being engaged with the work.

When you are engaged with the work, you care about it.

You spend time and energy - and brain power - focused on doing a better job and encouraging positive results from the work.

Some extra dollars on the paycheck doesn't accomplish this.

A worker can be satisfied with their pay - and even happy about it - without necessarily being productive at what they do.

EMPLOYEES ARE CATCHING ONTO THIS PROBLEM.

Adding to the complications is that employees are aware of this discrepancy.

Everyone wants to see employees more engaged in their work.

When surveyed, 89% of managers stated they want their employees to be more engaged with their work.

But when the employees were surveyed, 59% of them felt that the boss was too focused on finances.[4]

If your only perspective is money, you are going to lose productivity and employees.

When you simply pay more, you are showing to your team that you are doing the bare minimum to gain their loyalty.

Employees don't want the bare minimum.

They want to know that management cares about their health and their well-being.

Throwing money at the problem comes across as lazy - and ironically, disengaged from the employees.

And before you protest about that, know this...

IT IS YOUR PROBLEM TO FIX.

Some managers are tempted to feel like the disengaged employee has a problem that they need to figure out on their own.

"If they aren't happy with things, then they need to figure that out. I'm already paying them plenty!"

But direct managers are 70% of the variance in employee engagement[5], according to Gallup.

Whether you think it's an attitude problem or not, it's yours to fix.

But...

PAY IS A DECENT PLACE TO START.

Make no mistake about it, a fair paycheck is still a necessity if you want to boost morale.

When surveyed, 47% of employees do still believe they are underpaid.[6]

That's almost half the workforce unhappy with their paychecks!

If you decide to focus on increasing employee engagement, all the tactics in the world won't help your cause if your employees feel that they should be paid more money.

Is that confusing?

It doesn't have to be.

Just understand that your workers need to be paid fairly.

If your pay is competitive, then you can start working on other efforts to improve engagement.

But if you decide to implement new perks and install a ping-pong table in your office, but your employees feel that they are not being paid comparably to counterparts at other companies, then your efforts will actually do the opposite.

Think about it: if an employee is making 25% less with your company than similar workers at another company, he or she is not going to be happy that you are spending the company's budget on new kitchen appliances for the break room.

It's a balancing act.

Like everything else, you do need to consider your specific needs and circumstances.

In short, you have to actively engage with your employees to figure this one out.

If they aren't making a strong case for higher pay, then let's focus on ways that you can boost engagement without throwing money at it.

But if the prevailing view is that pay is low, you'll have to fix that first.

WHAT IF YOU KNOW YOU'RE PAYING FAIRLY?

Then you need to start working on new ways to engage your workforce. Active engagement, collaboration, and open communication will motivate employees to work harder and dedicate more time and focus to your company.

Create a collaborative think tank about culture within your organization that has multiple touches that essentially help with active engagement.

Analyze and survey your culture to understand, where are the shortfalls?

WHAT ABOUT ULTIMATE LOYALTY?

Something else to take into consideration is ultimate loyalty…

What's the ultimate loyalty that you can create within your work environment?

Ultimate loyalty is when you have emotional loyalty from your employees. They might like your brand, but you really want them to love your brand.

We want to create brand advocacy.

An employee can care about a brand, but do they really love it?

And how do you get them to love it?

How do you create that affinity for it?

And how do you create attachment?

By creating multiple touches, collaboration, and having open communication.

When you have the affinity and attachment, you can really create the trust where there's no barriers that is ultimate loyalty.

There's that deep love for the brand where you will go above and beyond merely what's asked of you because they have created an ecosystem.

A good engagement program has a good ecosystem where managers award or recognize their employees efforts.

Employees should have clear expectations when they start about what their roles and responsibilities are. They feel they are really truly informed about what the brand means and what the brand does.

The younger generation want to see, "Well, what are you doing for other people? How are you connecting in the community? And what are you doing for other people as a brand?"

And that's that love perspective.

That kind of brand love people really need to feel.

2

MYTH #2

WE DON'T HAVE THE TIME OR BUDGET!

As a business owner, your day is already packed.

You're managing your clients or your customers.

You have to keep employees on track.

You might be making sales.

Your job is to make sure everyone else's jobs are being done - and in some cases, you're doing those jobs, too.

The last thing you want to hear is, "There's another thing that you're responsible for!"

But when we talk about employee benefits packages and incentive programs that's exactly what managers hear.

It's hard to blame them.

If you're responsible for picking up the slack, then knowing that your company has to do something *else* is going to feel like a burden.

As we've already established, gone are the days when you can just cover retirement and healthcare and call it a day.

Employees expect perks and benefits in this day and age.

They want to know that they are valued members of the team, and benefits packages can do that.

WHAT DO THESE BENEFITS PACKAGES EVEN LOOK LIKE?

For some larger companies, expanding benefits packages is easy.

Any retail store is going to offer some kind of generous employee discount on their own products and services that may be enough to attract new recruits.

If your company has a partnership with other providers,

this can lead to other heavy discounts that might be beneficial to the employee.

Why do companies do this?

Well, it's easy to manage an internal employee discount program.

A blanket offering is straightforward, can be administered by giving either employees or cashiers some kind of discount code, and you can get back to business.

It doesn't take any chunk of time out of your already-packed workday.

It makes sense for everybody.

But what about younger businesses that don't have such a clear path to benefits?

What if you are an insurance provider?

Or a consultancy firm?

Or a marketing agency?

If you can't offer discounts on your own products or services, then it's time to get creative.

It's not uncommon for small to medium sized businesses to think outside the box with their benefits packages, hoping to attract and retain quality workers:

- Health and wellness programs designed to encourage employees to adopt a healthy and beneficial lifestyle which could reduce employer health care costs. <u>Employers can pay $3 to $7.5 per month per employee.</u>[1]
- Discount programs for other products and services, where employees can earn rewards that they can spend at their favorite retailers.
- Social recognition platforms that bring public acknowledgement of their hard work.
- Achievement awards that give tangible gifts for a hard working team.
- Expanded paid vacation offerings and paid time off, showing employees that work-life balance is an important piece of the puzzle.
- Big ticket discounts, so employees can earn credits towards expensive purchases they might not otherwise be able to afford.
- Tuition reimbursement and student loan payments, to encourage education and to help employees pay off the crippling student debt that they took on. A company can pay up to <u>$5,250 per year of their employees student debt.</u>[2]

These are all wonderful programs that benefit employees and companies.

But they come with one major problem.

THEY NEED TO BE MANAGED BY SOMEONE.

Take the "achievement award" idea.

On the surface, it seems simple enough: create an award and give it to someone when they are doing a good job to encourage more great performance.

But even a simple award like this comes with a number of jobs that you don't have time for:

- Coming up with the award idea.
- Producing the award itself.
- Communicating that award with the team.
- Creating the parameters for winning the award.
- Tracking those parameters so you're aware of everyone's job performance.
- Recognizing when someone has achieved enough to earn the award.
- Notifying that person that they have won the award.
- Distributing the award.

- Managing overtime.
- Staying relevant.

Now, some of these steps might only take a minute or two.

But it's another task on your already-full plate.

A bigger company might be able to handle this with their Human Resources department.

Or they might even establish a role for someone to be in charge of employee engagement and benefits.

You may not have enough in the budget to create an entirely new role or department purely for the purposes of keeping employees engaged.

And time is just one of the concerns with creating an engaging rewards program that bothers so many business owners...

HOW MUCH IS THIS GOING TO COST?

Think of a wellness program.

You want to encourage employees to take care of their health.

Makes total sense, doesn't it?

And it's an honorable behavior to incentivize.

An employee wellness program looks different for every team.

You might subsidize a gym membership for your workers.

Or you could create some on-site wellness sessions that employees can partake in, like yoga sessions or meditation groups.

This is good!

And you easily recognize this as an investment.

An employee that is taking care of his physical, emotional, and mental health is clearly going to be more productive for your company than one that isn't taking such good care of his or her own well-being.

Higher production.

Less sick days.

A more positive work environment.

The benefits pile up. Of course it's worth it.

Except...

A WELLNESS PROGRAM GETS EXPENSIVE QUICKLY.

Tight budgets are going to be a big problem for younger organizations who want to do something like this.

A wellness program can be costly, even with just a few benefits for your team.

The per-employee cost of a corporate wellness program has proven to be inconsistent at best.

Costs can be all over the place, depending on how extensive of a program you want to offer.

<u>Studies have shown it can cost between $150 and $1,200 per employee per year.</u>[3]

How are you supposed to budget for that when the costs vary that much?

If you're trying to estimate your costs for ten employees, that's the difference between finding an extra $1,500 and an extra $12,000 in the annual budget.

A big difference!

The key is customization.

HOW DIFFERENT CAN A BENEFITS PROGRAM BE?

Whether it's a wellness program or a performance-based rewards system, a benefits program can vary.

Let's stick with the health and wellness program as an example.

The higher end of the range - that $1,200 per employee per year number - is probably going to include a lot of different services and benefits for your team.

And any wellness program should be viewed as an investment, of course.

You are spending that money in hopes that you will get outsized profits in return from increased productivity and performance.

The list of included services in a high-end benefits program can get pretty long:

- Online health guides and resources.

- Integration with major fitness devices and smartwatches.
- Team challenges and rewards.
- Comprehensive wellness programs using proprietary platforms.
- Mobile apps and websites.
- Health risk appraisals.
- Incentive and rewards management.
- Full, planned wellness campaigns.
- Biometric screening.
- Telephonic health coaching and live chat support.

You need to make tough decisions that can include whittling away at this list until you have something that makes sense both for employee wellness and your bottom line.

You don't need all of those features.

But you do need to find a way to offer some of those features, potentially, in a way that won't break the bank or pull your time away from your typical duties as a manager.

Instead of throwing your hands in the air and assuming that you don't have the time or the budget to do something like this, you can look at outsourcing your benefits program to a company that specializes in it.

THE RIGHT QUESTIONS FOR A BENEFITS MANAGEMENT COMPANY.

This is the definition of "work smarter, not harder."

A benefits management company is going to make your benefits package far easier to handle, and it could save costs for you, too.

What a company or service will do is keep tabs on all the different time-consuming activities that come with a benefits program.

The company or service will track employee performance, issue rewards, or keep tabs on how the benefits are being administered.

If you're a manager, this is a no-brainer.

It takes the stress of administering a benefits program completely off your mind, while still preserving the benefits that your team can enjoy.

But like any third-party service, you need to ask a few basic questions to determine whether or not it's a good fit for your company, like:

- What is the cost of their service? Does it

make financial sense to outsource these benefits?
- How do they track and monitor the administration of those benefits? Is it transparent enough that you can keep an eye on them as an employer?
- Are they able to distribute rewards directly, or do they need to run every decision through the employer?
- Are they accessible on a regular basis in case anything goes wrong or you have a question?
- Can they help find new and exciting ways to increase benefits for employees while minimizing the costs to the company?

3

MYTH #3

REMOTE WORKERS ARE HARD TO MANAGE

I don't need to tell you that the COVID-19 pandemic of 2020 completely upended how we live and work.

Offices were forced to close all over the country.

But if you couldn't afford to cease operations altogether (who could?), then your team was thrust into a remote arrangement overnight.

In a lot of ways, this turned out to be a positive.

Many businesses learned that their teams could work from home and enjoy the same productivity - or even increased productivity - as a result.

Plus, remote workers aren't going to be using your office's electricity, water, or other resources.

Your costs to operate can go down significantly.

But as we also learned throughout this massive transition, the work environment becomes rife with new challenges.
Here are some powerful statistics from Prudential that share how the pandemic has impacted employees and their thoughts about their current employment.

- 26% of workers who plan to look for a job at a different company once the pandemic has subsided
- 75% of those who are planning to leave their jobs who say the pandemic made them rethink their skill sets
- 68% of American workers who say that having the ability to work both remotely and at the work site is the ideal workplace model
- 87% of workers among those who have been working remotely during the pandemic that want to[1]

ENGAGING EMPLOYEES FROM HOME JUST ISN'T THE SAME.

Let's say you have a sales team and you want to motivate them to stretch their sales goals for the week.

Engaging them with that goal requires a few different things: goal tracking and motivation, and the reward for the achievement.

If you work in your office together, it might not take much effort.

You can set up a whiteboard in one corner of the office, and everyone can track their sales there.

You could write down the goals for the team and illustrate their progress along the way.

You can even have regular announcements of the goal progress throughout each workday to refocus everyone on the task at hand.

As for the reward itself, the company can spring for a good pizza party or to have a big, catered lunch on Friday to thank the team for their hard work.

Giving everyone a little bit of a break where they can celebrate together improves camaraderie and morale, and everyone enjoys a little better attitude towards the company.

This is all great, and effective... *if you work in an office building together.*

If you've transformed your workplace to mainly a remote arrangement, then this sort of setup just isn't going to work for you, is it?

It's hard to create a motivating goal that everyone focuses on without having everyone there to talk to.

And throwing a pizza party or a catered lunch for the team is impossible when everyone is working from a different location!

But does that mean that engaging those employees is more difficult?

Not necessarily.

WORK ENVIRONMENT JUST HAS TO ADAPT TO NEW WORK ARRANGEMENTS.

As a manager, you have a particular way of working that has served you well - likely for years.

You might even borrow ideas from managers that you responded particularly well to over the years.

You visit employees at their desks, and you have regular check-ins with them to monitor their progress, offer a hearty handshake, and let them know that they are appreciated.

And of course, you like to reward them with catered meals or even office upgrades, like cappuccino machines in the break room, for example.

All of that goes out the window for your remote employees.

That's not a bad thing.

It just presents an opportunity for you to adjust your approach.

Remote workers are not inherently any harder to manage than on-site employees. In fact, they might be a little easier.

ALL EMPLOYEES ARE LOOKING FOR THE SAME THINGS.

When you separate on-site and remote workers in your mind, then you are tempted to treat them differently on a high level.

But I just said that you need to adapt your approach.

Wouldn't that mean treating employees differently?

Am I contradicting myself?

Not necessarily.

At the end of the day, employees are all looking for the same things:

- **Appreciation** - recognition that their hard work does not go unnoticed.
- **Connection** - some kind of meaningful relationship with their boss and/or coworkers.
- **Personalization** - benefits that address their needs and desires.
- **Recognition** - the understanding that their concerns are heard, validated, and being addressed.

You can see how these things are rather easily handled in an office environment, but how they can fall by the wayside in a remote working arrangement.

MANY CONCERNS COME DOWN TO COMMUNICATION.

Keeping your remote workers happy and engaged with the job can be done with two simple steps.

The first is open communication.

Fortunately, in today's world, open communication is rather simple to achieve.

With online communication platforms like Slack, you can instantaneously and regularly check in with teammates and get questions answered quickly.

Even a quick Zoom or Google Meet call can work wonders.

When you are proactive in your communication with your remote workers, you are going to increase the chances that they will be engaged with their work.

But at the end of the day, you still need to provide ways to increase emotional loyalty, which is the second step.

EMOTIONAL LOYALTY: THE SECRET INGREDIENT TO REMOTE WORKER ENGAGEMENT.

How do you build emotional loyalty with a remote team?

If you can build an engagement system that will motivate them to engage with their work, you can still reap the benefits of a remote arrangement with the high engagement that you get from your office workers.

Easier said than done, of course.

A good engagement system to promote emotional loyalty will include the following:

- Communicate clear expectations.
- Establish open communications among peers.
- Invite peers to collaborate on projects.
- Measure employee performance.
- Hold employees accountable.

That sounds like a lot of work!

And much like working with an engagement system in the office, without the right tools, you could find yourself having to spend more time and/or money than you would like on managing this sort of system.

That is, unless you *did* have the right tools.

4

MYTH #4

MILLENNIALS ARE JUST NEEDY

You know you've heard it before. Maybe you've even said it.

Millennials.

In some circles, that's a curse word.

The reputation of millennials has taken a hit in recent years.

The older generations feel that millennials are entitled, needy, and force everyone to coddle them.

On the surface, this is really hard to argue.

There are absolutely problems with keeping millennials on the job.

And this is an even bigger problem than you might think, considering millennials are the largest generation in our workforce today.[1]

THEY'RE JOB-HOPPERS BECAUSE THEY HAVE NO EMOTIONAL LOYALTY TO THE COMPANY.

The classic view of a career is as follows: a guy gets an entry-level job in the mailroom of a big firm.

He works hard and builds his reputation in the company, moves up to an assistant role.

Then he gets a supervisor role.

Then a management role.

Within a decade, he's upper-management.

He becomes a fixture of the company until his retirement, where he gets a nice gold watch as a gift for his years of service.

Now, let's look at the stereotypical millennial approach to a career: a guy gets an entry-level job in the mail room.

He gets impatient, demanding more from his job than his bosses are willing or able to give him.

He loses patience with it, quits, and moves into a different role that he feels will serve him better.

Repeat as desired.

While the facts are fairly accurate, this is not necessarily the cut-and-dry situation as you might think.

One piece of this is definitely true: millennials are three times more likely to switch jobs than any other age group, according to Gallup.[2]

Of course, this is the kiss of death for any group of employees.

Despite being very knowledgeable, skilled, and talented, employers fear hiring millennials because why put all the time, effort, and money into hiring and retaining someone if they are more likely to walk away at the first sign of trouble?

The key is understanding *why* they are walking away… and then you can figure out how to keep them with you.

WHY ARE MILLENNIALS SWITCHING JOBS?

There is a great snippet in Gallup's analysis of millennials in the workforce, titled, How Millennials Want to Work and Live:[3]

Compared with those from other generations, Millennials are as satisfied or more satisfied with nearly all aspects of their job. Gallup uncovered this trend in a recent analysis of three overarching job aspects:

1. ***The tangible rewards a job brings****;*
2. ***The demands a job imposes on a person****;*
3. ***The opportunities a job offers****.*

So if Millennials are as satisfied as older generations, why are they so likely to switch jobs? Because "job satisfaction" (measured by the three aspects noted above) isn't the same as engagement at work."

Re-read that last line again: "'Job satisfaction' isn't the same as engagement at work.'" That is what you need to know, not just about millennials, but about the workforce in general.

Most employers are focused on job satisfaction. But

even if there's nothing wrong with a job, an employee may still be not as engaged as they could be.

There's your problem.

WHY DO THESE THINGS DISENGAGE A MILLENNIAL?

Engagement is a deeper emotional connection and loyalty to a job and a company.

It implies that someone working for you feels a sense of pride and connection in the job that they do for you.

They have ownership of that job, and that is what drives them.

If any employee feels that they are simply in a rut, doing the same job every day, over and over, without any real advancement, then they will feel disengaged from the work.

There is no reason to engage with it because the work doesn't provide any reason to.

The same is true for the lack of a job opportunity.

This speaks to the engagement an employee has with the company.

Any worker is looking for advancement in their job.

They want to know that their hard work is leading somewhere.

If they are working hard because they know it will lead to the next level of employment, then you will see them far more engaged with the process.

Think about that: when someone is challenged at work, and they know that rising above those challenges and conquering them will advance their careers, you have to know that they are going to be more engaged.

But the third piece of the puzzle is very important: the tangible rewards a job brings.

TANGIBLE REWARDS ARE NOT JUST ABOUT MONEY OR "FUN" PERKS.

Companies are so susceptible to overthinking this step… or underthinking it.

Let's start with underthinking it.

Employers like to give raises and bonuses.

These are great motivators - at least, for a little while.

Everyone wants to earn more money, and I don't know a single worker who will turn down a raise if offered one.

But the engagement you get from a worker for a raise offers limited returns over time.

Once an employee settles in with their new salary, it's going to be difficult to get them to re-engage.

After all, the new salary is now the "new normal," so it stops being a motivating factor.

Besides that, there is a limit to how many times you can reasonably give someone a raise, which makes it more difficult to employ that strategy in the long term.

For overthinking, companies try really hard to be "fun."

They spend money on foosball tables for the break room, or gourmet appliances in the kitchen.

And while this is great to a point, it's also - again - going to offer diminishing returns.

Once your team is used to the slide next to the escalator,

then it becomes less a "benefit" and more a "thing that's always there."

Making your workplace like a theme park is fine.

But if you work at a theme park, it starts to feel less like a theme park over time.

When millennials are looking for tangible rewards, it's not them feeling entitled.

They just want acknowledgement that their hard work is benefiting the company and is recognized.

How you do this is important - and can be different depending on the workplace.

5

MYTH #5

ENGAGEMENT ISN'T THAT IMPORTANT

It is very easy to take on a poor attitude when thinking about actively considering employee engagement.

Especially if you come from a previous generation and you always took pride in work well done no matter what, it can be difficult to think that it is your responsibility to keep your employees engaged.

And when you also are worried about keeping costs under control, making sure clients or customers are satisfied, keeping operations going, and managing the other two dozen responsibilities that come from being management, employee engagement falls down the list rather quickly.

But that's precisely the problem - and when your employees aren't engaged, your whole business suffers.

Building a strong company culture of engaged workers doesn't happen automatically.

But if you can put forth the effort to do it the right way, you'll create a workforce of happy, satisfied employees that will engage with others, promote your brand, become evangelists for your product, and will work hard to increase their productivity.

Isn't that what any manager wants? How many of your other problems would disappear if you had that?

A recent study showed employees that were engaged outperform those disengaged by over 200%.[1] Imagine getting that kind of improvement out of your team!

HOW DO YOU INCREASE ENGAGEMENT?

The temptation is to immediately think of money.

As we've discussed already in this guide, money isn't everything. It can't motivate employees long-term.

It becomes a never ending cycle of unsustainable raises, and soon you're paying more than you can and still not achieving the results that you are looking for.

Rather, what you want is to build up a culture that engages your employees on a more sustainable basis.

And the more you work on this, the more natural, effective, and productive it will be.

START WITH OPPORTUNITIES FOR DEVELOPMENT.

Companies that invest in training for their employees see their profit margins outperform those that don't by 24%.[2]

In other words, spend time developing your employees!

Truth is, today, workers feel as though they're not really achieving what they are setting out to do with their jobs.

A full 74% of employees in one survey said they weren't reaching their full potential at work[3] because they felt there weren't as many opportunities for development.

There are plenty of ways you can remedy this quickly and efficiently, including:

- Developing individual training plans based on an employee's goals. This is something you may already know based on onboarding

interviews, but you may have to sit down with each team member and discuss where they want their careers to go. Creating some kind of rough road map for them can go a long way in engaging them in their work because they will feel that they are headed in a particular direction.
- Providing regular check-ins, mentorship, and training to employees goes right along with this.
- Offer opportunities for training on a regular basis to help them develop essential skills, like leadership training, for example. But the key in doing so is providing explanation and inspiration for them to attend and engage with these training sessions. Show them *why* these sessions are valuable and what they can do to further their careers.

None of this is rocket science.

And yes, there are other ways that we will get to.

But it's important to understand the foundation of what we are doing when we provide engagement for our employees.

They need to know that they have a direction.

They also need to trust their leadership (you).

PROVIDE STRONG, TRANSPARENT LEADERSHIP.

How common is the stereotype that management doesn't know what they are doing?

The movie *Office Space* turned this into an art form: managers didn't communicate well with employees, creating a political minefield and making everyone miserable when they worked in the office.

Unfortunately, the reason that movie was so funny is because it was so true.

Many management teams are very disconnected from their workforce.

This doesn't mean you have to be buddies with everyone that walks through the door.

But your workers do need to trust you.

And they don't: 58% of respondents in one survey[4] said they trusted a total stranger more than their own boss.

No matter what perks you provide to your team, you're

not going to get a more engaged workforce in that environment.

The good news is that you can heal this problem with a few simple steps, like:

- Open, reciprocal communication.
- Solid benefits and compensation (more on this in a moment).
- Job security.
- Deliver on promises made to staff (this is a big one!).
- Work ethically.

This isn't complicated, but it is important, and if you can be a boss that your team respects and trusts, you'll get even greater rewards out of the next tip.

OFFER SMART, CUSTOMIZED INCENTIVES.

Rewarding employees for increased performance at their jobs is a fantastic way to build engagement among your team.

But we've all worked for companies that offered the wrong rewards.

Rather, learn what your team wants and then find ways to provide that for them.

Customize the incentives and you'll see outsized results.

Gallup estimates that up to 70% of employees feel disengaged from their work because of a lack of incentives.[5]

That is a massive number!

But how do you provide those customized incentives?

For one thing, take the time to learn more about your team.

And think about where they are in their lives.

They might respond better to some benefits than others.

EMPLOYEE BENEFITS CREATE ENGAGEMENT THE MOST.

Offering benefits to your employees above and beyond the paycheck is a strong way to build a healthy company culture, and it is definitely the most effective over time.

With an attractive benefits package, you create loyalty and pride among your employees.

Why?

With a benefits package, you send a clear message to your workers that you value their health and their future.

When you simply give a raise, you are just throwing money at an issue.

Benefits are far more engaging.

Plus, this helps you differentiate your business from competitors who are looking to hire away your best talent - it's almost like an insurance policy for your staff.

STRONG ENGAGEMENT IMPROVES OFFICE CULTURE AND ATMOSPHERE.

If your workers are stressed out just at the thought of setting foot in your office building, then something is wrong.

If they cringe at having to face their coworkers, your culture is
off.

Build a team and a culture around keeping things relaxed and finding ways to have fun with the job.

It doesn't mean your office has to be an 8-hour-long party every day.

That will come across as forced and fake.

The last thing you want is to be insincere with your team.

People can detect that a mile away, and if you force it, it will have the opposite effect - and it will harm the already-delicate relationship you have with them as management.

But providing ways for workers to relax and interact with each other in a positive way, and building a reputation for open communication and feedback among everyone will take much greater strides in improving your culture.

And along that same thinking...

YOUR POSITION AS THE BOSS NEEDS TO BE UNDERSTOOD.

I don't mean this from the "my way or the highway"

perspective.

Employees will have a complicated relationship with the boss.

They will respect you if you set clear parameters for your office, of course.

The work is important.

Your business is important.

Those are things you have to take seriously.

But don't take yourself too seriously.

Be willing to talk with your employees.

Crack a few jokes.

If you don't like joking around, just be personable and pleasant.

Be friendly.

Be willing to laugh.

And be authentic.

There is a balance of putting forth a strong effort in your work and also recognizing that everyone is human and we can all "take a chill pill" sometimes.

Fun, goofy rewards can help with that.

And if you're the boss, don't be afraid to allow everyone to have a few laughs at your expense.

By humanizing yourself, you will build more loyalty with your workers… as long as you are sincere.

CREATE AN ATMOSPHERE THAT ENCOURAGES QUESTIONS.

You're not born knowing how to do your job.

It's something you learn over time.

That principle needs to be a guide when you are dealing with your employees.

That means, first, having patience while they learn the job.

If they are a strong fit for your organization, then they will get the hang of it eventually.

Be okay with a few mistakes here and there - that's how people learn.

If you can create a culture where it's okay to ask questions about what you don't know, you can find those weak points and shore them up.

Along with that, extra training and guidance for those who need it is always going to pay off for you.

Investing that time can help employees turn the corner and become strong contributors.

BE GENEROUS WITH THOSE PERKS AND REWARDS.

Remember: everyone wants to be rewarded for a job well done.

If you can create a rewards system that incentivizes good performance, you can really make a big difference in the productivity of your team as a whole.

Don't be stingy or make the terms and parameters too strict.

You want your team to stretch, but you also want them to feel as though the goals are achievable.

6

MYTH #6

GIFT CARDS ARE THE BEST INCENTIVE!

One of your salespeople just hit their monthly goal.

Great!

As their boss, you want them to know that they are appreciated - and you want to motivate them to keep hitting those goals in the future.

So you stop by their desk and drop off an Amazon Gift Card for $50.

You pat them on the shoulder, flash a smile, and thank them for their hard work.

As you stroll away from their desk, you might feel very satisfied with yourself.

After all, this employee put in extra hours to hit those numbers.

That gift card was an extra expense to the company, and it feels good to give a little extra.

You're being a great boss, right?

Unfortunately, what you don't realize is that your star salesperson looked at that gift card, shrugged their shoulders, tossed it on their desk, and went back to work as usual.

I bet the boss thinks they did a great job, they might be thinking.

Now, let's get one thing clear: it's not that this salesperson is ungrateful or selfish.

It's just that gift cards aren't as strong of a motivational tool as many employers think - and certainly not in the way that they are being used.

GIFT CARDS ARE BIG BUSINESS FOR EMPLOYERS.

There is no arguing the popularity of gift cards to employers in this day and age.

Companies in the United States alone spend $24 billion annually on gift cards[1] to motivate their employees.

They are far and away the most prevalent kind of employee reward being used in workplaces.

And if everyone is doing the same thing, there must be some power in it, right?

There are absolutely times when a gift card is the best option available to a company.

But often, they just aren't a good fit - and could be *demotivating* your employees.

First, let's review why so many are using them.

GIFT CARDS ARE CONVENIENT REWARDS.

The number one reason why anyone is using gift cards is that they are convenient.

It's the same reason many people use gift cards for birthday presents or Christmas gift exchanges: *it's just so easy.*

And as an employer, you have a lot on your plate already.

Managing your team is a tall order, so being able to have a stack of gift cards at the ready whenever you need them is a surefire way to keep it simple.

GIFT CARDS DON'T PLAY FAVORITES.

The last thing you want to do is look as though you appreciate one employee more than another.

Playing favorites is a quick way to distance yourself from your staff and frustrate them into a large loss of productivity.

And even if your intentions are good, buying rewards can sometimes appear lopsided.

It doesn't matter how much you spend if the value looks different for one reward versus another.

With gift cards, you can give the same value every time.

If everyone is getting a gift card worth $50 when they perform well, then there are no accusations that anyone is being favored unfairly.

Gift cards level the playing field.

GIFT CARDS LET THE EMPLOYEES REWARD THEMSELVES.

Instead of trying to please everyone, gift cards let everyone please themselves.

If you have a diverse team of employees who might be motivated by very different things, then it can become a chore to try and figure out what rewards would work best for each worker - while ensuring that it doesn't appear as though you're playing favorites!

Again, you don't have extra time to be managing this.

By rewarding with gift cards, you are still providing value while allowing the worker to pick out their own reward.

You can be confident that they are going to like what they get because they are the ones buying them.

As you can see, there are definitely some upsides to using gift cards for a rewards system.

However, the same things that provide advantages for gift cards are the same things that can be viewed as negatives in different contexts.

And when they are viewed as negatives, not only do they fail at motivating employees, they may also cause your employees to *not* work as hard as they can - defeating the purpose of rewarding them in the first place!

GIFT CARDS CAN BE VERY IMPERSONAL.

Perhaps the number one problem with gift cards is just how bland they are.

Just like when a husband buys his wife a gift card to a store for their wedding anniversary, a boss getting a gift card for an employee might be nice, but it also doesn't really demonstrate any kind of effort.

The result is that you're out the expense of the gift card and the worker doesn't feel any more appreciated than they were before.

If it's a gift card you just give to anyone who does well, where is the feeling of personal appreciation?

GIFT CARDS ARE LARGELY FORGETTABLE.

You'd remember the day that the boss rewarded your team with new iPads.

You won't remember the day the boss rewarded you with gift cards.

Why not?

There's nothing distinctive about a gift card. It's bland.

The fact that it is so flexible also contributes to this.

It can be used for anything, so it isn't really viewed as anything.

When you reward your employees, you want it to be a moment that motivates them - something they can think about when they have to work hard again in the future, knowing that there is a reward in it for them if they reach those benchmarks.

But if you just give them gift cards, there's often nothing tangible about that reward that they can remember and think about to motivate themselves in the future.

GIFT CARDS OFFER NO ACCOUNTABILITY.

Unless you take the time to keep detailed written records yourself, there really is no tracking who receives gift cards, how much, how often, and when.

Part of a rewards system is tracking, so that you know who are the top performers and can analyze who needs more attention or more guidance.

With a stack of gift cards in your desk drawer, you don't get any of that accountability.

You might as well just be giving them cash.

GIFT CARDS COULD BE TOO NARROW.

In an attempt to keep it more memorable, you might be tempted to try to get a specific gift card instead.

In other words, instead of just a general gift card, you give one for a store like Target, Best Buy, or Macy's.

This can be even worse than giving a generic gift card.

By picking a store and limiting yourself, you're also running the risk of alienating employees that frankly aren't interested in the reward.

Best Buy is a great example.

There is plenty to purchase at Best Buy.

Everyone needs electronics and gadgets, so this could be a big win for your team.

And maybe it is for most of them.

But there will always be some employees who aren't exactly thrilled about the reward.

Why?

Because they don't watch DVDs, they just got a new TV, they have a year and a half left on their phone plans, and the reward isn't big enough to buy a new laptop.

So they're stuck with a gift card to a store that they aren't even going to bother shopping at.

If they aren't interested in the reward, they're not going to be motivated to work any harder, will they?

And related to this...

SMALLER GIFT CARD AMOUNTS CAN FRUSTRATE EMPLOYEES.

You don't have room in your budget to issue $500 gift cards to everyone on the team when they hit their sales numbers.

Few companies have that kind of spending money.

But if you keep it low, like $25, you might not motivate that many people.

Sure, $25 is a nice gesture, but to enjoy it, the employee is probably going to have to spend some of their own money.

It's not $25, it's a $25 reward if they spend more than that.

Nobody wants that.

Where is the line?

You'd have to figure that out - both for your budget and for your employees... and it might not be that clear.

SO WHAT DO WE DO NOW?

If gift cards are that terrible of a motivator, should we just ignore them altogether?

No.

Like any method of rewarding your workers, gift cards can be effective if you use them the right way.

The key is building a plan that allows your team to build up rewards as they work, and allows them to redeem those rewards on things that they will actually want.

And being able to customize each reward for each employee can be a huge motivating factor for disillusioned and unappreciated workers.

7

MYTH #7

INCENTIVE PROGRAMS TAKE CARE OF THEMSELVES!

When a company puts together a benefits package, like health insurance, there isn't a lot of management that goes into it beyond that initial setup.

Sometimes there are issues, but overall, it runs on autopilot:

- You pick the particular plan that you want for your employees.
- You get everyone signed up.
- And the program basically takes care of itself.

An employee goes to the doctor and the plan already has a process for handling it.

It's a very hands-off situation, for the most part.

It's tempting, then, for employers like you to assume that an employee engagement program would be just as hands-off.

THIS IS WHAT WE ALL WANT FROM AN ENGAGEMENT PROGRAM, RIGHT?

As the boss, your job goes far beyond just setting up employee incentive programs.

Yes, you need to ensure your workers are taken care of.

You are responsible for their development, their productivity, and the output of your team as a whole.

But there are probably other decisions that you are making every single day.

You're dealing with interpersonal communications and relationships; you might be dealing with clients, processing orders, and making high-level decisions for the company and/or your team.

Managing an incentive program is something that you would want to be on autopilot, too, right?

Yet, you can't let that happen for a few reasons.

REASON #1: AN ENGAGEMENT PROGRAM HAS TO EVOLVE WITH YOUR TEAM

Just because you set up a system for rewarding your employees doesn't mean it will work for the rest of your career.

Times change, and teams change.

If you keep the same employees for years at a time, their needs and desires could evolve as they get older and their lives change.

An employee that is in their mid-twenties and single will be looking for different incentives than an employee in their thirties who is married with two children.

For that reason alone, you need to regularly manage your incentive program regularly and make sure you are offering things that motivate your employees.

Teams change in other ways too, of course.

If you have turnover in your company, the new team members that come in could be from a completely different generation, background, or makeup than the ones that they are replacing.

They need different motivations to keep themselves productive.

And let's not forget about the times changing. Society evolves and can be completely different overnight.

Let's say you normally reward your employees with gift cards to dine out at local restaurants.

In large parts of 2020, that type of reward likely wouldn't motivate employees - there's no reason to work hard for a gift card to a place that isn't open for customers!

So you always need to be paying close attention to your reward offerings, adapting them for the people and the environment around you.

REASON #2: OUT OF SIGHT, OUT OF MIND

If a tree falls in the forest and nobody is around to hear it, does it make a sound?

If an incentive program offers rewards to employees, but nobody pays attention to it, does it make a difference?

You can have the best rewards system around, but if

nobody notices it, it's not doing anything for you or your team.

When an incentive program gets stale, it stops motivating anybody to improve their performance.

Employees become bored with it, and it is just another thing that is a part of your company and blends into the background.

This happens often with incentive programs when they don't evolve with teams and circumstances.

If you let your incentive program sit too long, it stops incentivizing.

BUT YOU DON'T HAVE THE TIME OR ENERGY TO KEEP UPDATING YOUR ENGAGEMENT PROGRAM.

As we stated in the start of this chapter, managing your engagement program is something that takes time and energy.

When you are managing your team and your business, keeping your engagement program humming along is not something that you're able to do long term.

Doing a half-baked job won't help, either.

And you don't have the budget to outsource this to another position.

Hiring someone to manage your incentive program is costly and unnecessary.

So are we stuck?

Is there no solution that addresses these problems without a heavy investment in time and/or money?

WHICH ENGAGEMENT PROGRAM WILL YOU INTEGRATE TODAY?

When you get these false beliefs out of your way, you hold the power to ramp up employee morale and boost your bottom line.

The easiest way to do that is by utilizing our patented rewards platform, COGZ™ Recognition Rewards.

- It's customizable.
- It's affordable (and costs nothing to use to get started).
- It's easy to set up.
- It makes your rewards system an automatic no-brainer.
- And most importantly, it works.

MYTH 1 & 2: WHY COGZ ELIMINATES THE "TIME/BUDGET" CONCERN FOR YOU.

The patented COGZ Recognition Rewards platform allows you to track your employee's goals and incentives in one central location, customized to whatever it is you are trying to incentivize.

Using the COGZ system, you can issue rewards, track them, and adapt your offerings over time.

You can issue discounts and gift cards, or you can provide fitness trackers.

You can even give them the option to take cash rewards.

Regardless of your needs, COGZ can be tailored for you.

There are no upfront costs, and it only takes minutes to set up.

No more stressing about schedules, and no more worrying about budgets.

You just get to enjoy the increased productivity and engagement from your team, thanks to a quality rewards system that you don't even have to manage yourself.

To keep the time and financial costs of a benefits program down for the highest return on investment for your company, you may look to COGZ coins from Boost Engagement.

MYTH #3: WHY COGZ RECOGNITION REWARDS IS THE RIGHT TOOL FOR THE JOB.

Some managers will think that the struggle to engage remote workers is too much.

They may not accept not allowing their team to work remotely, forcing them to come in (though in some areas of the world right now, that is not an option).

Or, they will allow remote workers and just roll the dice, hoping that the employees will be engaged on their own, somehow.

With COGZ Recognition Rewards, you don't have to settle.

The beauty of the patented COGZ Recognition Rewards system is its flexibility.

Now, we know that COGZ offers exceptional flexibility not just from a budgetary standpoint.

It is simple to build a custom incentive structure that will fit your team and your bottom line.

But in addition to this, COGZ also allows you to offer this high level of engagement to your remote workers.

Being a unique hybrid combination of cloud-based and tangible awards, COGZ is a platform that can measure your workers' performance no matter where they are working.

In other words, the playing field is level: remote workers and in-house workers can have the same incentive structure, and they are measured the same way.

You empower yourself to handle your team's productivity anywhere they are.

And this customization is key.

In a typical office setting, you might hand out a gift card to an employee, or present them with a traveling award.

But with COGZ, you can allow your team to earn their rewards remotely.

When they reach those milestones - which are measured and recorded with the COGZ platform automatically -

then the system can distribute the rewards and notify you of the employee's performance.

Speaking of that notification...

ACCOUNTABILITY - EVEN FOR REMOTE WORKERS

Accountability is one of those things that is very frustrating for the average manager of remote workers.

How do you know they are staying on task?

With COGZ, you can set up the system to measure whatever metrics you want.

If you want to ensure that each employee is held to the same standard of performance, you can build that into your system.

That way, all employees - remote or onsite - are responsible for hitting their benchmarks every day.

It makes accountability easy because it provides reporting for you to review.

You can know exactly how your remote workers are

performing at a glance without having to check in with each one individually.

Plus, this makes the job easier for remote employees because you are laying down the guidelines and parameters for a successful job.

This allows them the ability to manage their workday in a way that will deliver results because they have clear goals to aspire to.

In other words, COGZ solves the accountability and incentive problem that keeps so many remote employees disengaged from their jobs.

SET IT UP ONCE AND JUST LET IT RUN

Being proactive is key for many managers trying to deliver results for their company.

With COGZ Recognition Rewards, you are able to solve a lot of challenges and issues with just a few clicks of your mouse or trackpad.

You don't need any special experience or skills to get it done - you just set it up and let it do the heavy lifting.

It doesn't take long, either: with prebuilt templates that

you can manage metrics and customize awarding reasons for your evolving needs, you can create the incentive program that remote workers and onsite workers alike will respond well to, so that you can have an engaged workforce doing their absolute best for the company.

MYTH #4: REMOVE THIS MYTH BY CUSTOMIZING THE REWARDS FOR YOUR TEAM - AND KEEP THEM ENGAGED WITH A SOCIAL PLATFORM.

The best way to implement a rewards system in your workplace is by knowing your team first.

Know what kinds of rewards they like. Understand what motivates them.

Pay attention to their interests and what would lead them to engage with the work more effectively.

Now, how can you do this?

There are a number of ways, like surveying your team.

But there is a way that you can do it automatically, while simultaneously incentivizing the productivity of your team.

COGZ Recognition Rewards offers a lot of flexibility for the employer, but it also offers ways to be flexible for the employee.

When you set up COGZ for the first time, you can set the parameters for what behavior or results you want to see improved in your team (and you can easily set this up with one of the pre-built templates, saving you loads of time).

Once you set this up, you could choose to award rewards points to your team when they reach their milestones.

Then, they can redeem these points for rewards of their own choosing.

By doing it this way, you can immediately start improving the performance of your team with motivating rewards, and at the same time, you are going to learn what motivates them and what leads them to greater productivity.

How?

By letting them choose their own rewards for a while.

Whenever a team member redeems a reward, you'll know about it.

You can study the history of rewards redemptions and make decisions on future rewards based on what they are choosing.

It's like a live survey, but your team gets to reap the benefits of it immediately.

And your company will as well, because they have to earn those rewards from the start.

And with a dedicated social platform built right in, your team can keep track of everyone's achievements and compete to move up the leaderboard.

It's just one of the many ways COGZ Recognition Rewards offers flexibility that you can take advantage of to build a system that works for your team.

FLEXIBILITY *DOESN'T* COME AT A COST

What's great is that this flexibility does not cost extra.

In fact, you actually get to implement this game plan without spending a dime.

With COGZ Recognition Rewards, you don't have to pay for anything until an employee earns a milestone.

In this way, you can take the system for a test drive, customizing it and adapting it as you go along, and you can offer a lot for your team without having to take on a financial risk.

You see, millennials aren't just needy.

There seems to be a disconnect between the modern working generation and the companies and management that employ them.

If you can take active steps to engage with that workforce and understand them on a deeper level, you can create a working environment that will retain workers effortlessly.

COGZ Recognition Rewards makes that easy for you.

MYTH #5: REMOVE THIS MYTH THROUGH GENEROSITY.

One simple way to do this is with Boost Engagement's patented COGZ Recognition Rewards system, now in its 2.0 offering.

With this revised and improved system, you can easily and conveniently offer unique rewards to your employees at a price that makes sense for everybody - and you can do it in just a few minutes.

MYTH #6: REMOVE THIS MYTH WITH OUR COGZ SOFTWARE

Instead of hiring an extra employee who has to manage the rewards system full-time (and it sure seems like it would be a full-time job to remember all of these things!), you can implementCOGZ Recognition Rewards.[1]

With our customizable rewards system, you can activate a clear path to rewards for your employees that will be geared specifically to them.

And rather than having to spend hours building it, you can use a pre-made template to start quickly and easily.

The result will be a far more motivated team who will feel appreciated for the work that they are doing, because their management cares enough to pay attention to what they want.

You don't want your employees to think that you only care about how much you're spending.

Putting in a little extra effort can make all the difference

- and with COGZ Recognition Rewards, that extra effort doesn't take much at all.

MYTH #7: REMOVE THIS MYTH THROUGH COGZ RECOGNITION REWARDS HANDLING YOUR PROBLEMS FOR YOU.

COGZ Recognition Rewards is unique in its offering to businesses because we have special features that keep these problems from arising - without costing you an arm and a leg.

First, with easy-to-use templates and other adaptable features (even including ways for employees to build their own incentive programs), your incentive program doesn't have to sit and be stale.

It can continue to be effective in the long term because it is easy to freshen up as you need to.

You retain the full control over the program and can administer new benefits with a few clicks, if you want.

The second program is even more important - and COGZ has unique and effective solutions for it.

To keep your incentive program from growing stale, COGZ Recognition Rewards offers two great features.

The first one is the trophy stack.

Each employee will be able to earn rewards that offer visual reminders of what they've won with their job performance.

Over time, this stack grows, reminding the employee of their achievements and motivating them to continue working hard to reach benchmarks.

By doing this, they will be motivated to "gamify" their development as workers, pushing themselves to be better so that they can win more awards.

The second one is equally motivating: the social platform.

With COGZ Recognition Rewards, your employees have a special portal online where they connect with each other.

This further enhances the "gaming" nature of the program.

By connecting to this platform, employees can see a news feed where they are updated with their coworkers' achievements and rewards earned, allowing them to compete with each other.

There are leaderboards, announcement feeds, and ways to easily be notified of new rewards being offered (which again, can be done in minutes with COGZ).

ENGAGEMENT WITH THE WORK IS ONLY HALF THE BATTLE.

To continuously motivate your employees to work harder for their rewards, they don't just need to be engaged with their work.

They need to be engaged with their rewards program.

With these social features and fun ways to motivate your employees, your team will continually be encouraged to engage with the platform, work for more achievements, and develop their skillset.

And when they do all of these things, your company benefits.

Remember: COGZ Recognition Rewards makes this very easy - so that you can prevent your rewards program from becoming stale and forgettable - at an affordable price without taking up too much of your time.

COGZ™ RECOGNITION CURRENCY
INSPIRE. ENGAGE. IMPACT.

Over 44.2 million people have filed for unemployment since the start of the Covid-19 pandemic. And since May 2020, more than 100,000 small businesses went bankrupt indefinitely. To make matters worse, the few who managed to stay afloat must now do so with a distracted, afraid, and compromised remote workforce. Something 98% of small businesses were not prepared or equipped to handle in such short notice. Were you one of them?

It's not your fault. If you implement what we've shared in this book, you will build a recession-proof framework for your business that enabled us to 10x our annual output and sales in just one month *during* the worst pandemic the world has ever seen.

We know there's nothing like our rewards program in the world, and we've even patented many of the features, processes, and ideas that make it truly a one-of-a-kind tool to empower your company culture, boost your workforce engagement, and skyrocket your sales growth in a very short period of time.

We believe this so much that we're willing to give you access to our patented software for a full 60 days to test it out and see for yourself - for FREE!

We know that when you implement COGZ™ Rewards in your business you will experience radical improvement and growth in just 30 days.

Want to receive your free access code to our rewards program or see it in action before making the small step of faith for your business? You can learn more about COGZ™ Recognition Currency at:

Boost Engagement with COGZ Coins.
https://culture.hr

ABOUT ANITA EMOFF

As Chairman and Owner of Boost Engagement, Anita oversees operations and sets the example for a driven, positive culture for the company.

Her passionate personality brings out the best in her

organization and staff. Both Anita and her husband Michael have been critical leaders in designing new technology solutions for their clients.

With over 20 years of sales and management experience, Anita has led Boost Engagement to become one of the 50 Fastest Growing Women-Owned Businesses in the world (2011-2016).

ENDNOTES

YOU'VE BEEN DUPED!

1. https://www.greatplacetowork.com.hk/wp-content/uploads/2019/04/2019-fortune-100-best-trends-employee-experience-at-the-best-workplaces-in-america-2.pdf

1. MYTH #1

1. https://www.perkbox.com/uk/resources/library/interactive-the-financial-cost-of-employee-disengagement
2. https://www.perkbox.com/uk/resources/library/interactive-the-financial-cost-of-employee-disengagement
3. http://www.diva-portal.org/smash/get/diva2:832968/FULLTEXT01.pdf
4. https://www.perkbox.com/uk/resources/library/interactive-the-financial-cost-of-employee-disengagement
5. https://www.perkbox.com/uk/resources/library/interactive-the-financial-cost-of-employee-disengagement
6. https://addisongroup.com/insights/insight/what-makes-employees-head-for-the-hills/?preview=true&_thumbnail_id=31487

2. MYTH #2

1. https://www.passporthealthusa.com/employer-solutions/blog/2019-5-how-much-do-wellness-programs-cost/
2. https://www.usnews.com/education/blogs/student-loan-ranger/articles/how-second-stimulus-bill-affects-employer-student-loan-repayment-benefit
3. https://www.passporthealthusa.com/employer-solutions/blog/2019-5-how-much-do-wellness-programs-cost/

3. MYTH #3

1. https://news.prudential.com/presskits/pulse-american-worker-survey-is-this-working.htm

4. MYTH #4

1. http://www.pewresearch.org/fact-tank/2015/05/11/millennials-surpass-gen-xers-as-the-largest-generation-in-u-s-labor-force/
2. http://www.gallup.com/businessjournal/211799/trends-disrupt-workplace-forever.aspx?utm_source=alert&utm_medium=email&utm_content=morelink&utm_campaign=syndication
3. http://www.gallup.com/reports/189830/millennials-work-live.aspx?utm_source=gbj&utm_medium=copy&utm_campaign=20170608-gbj

5. MYTH #5

1. https://www.dalecarnegie.com/employee-engagement/engaged-employees-infographic/
2. https://www.go-gulf.ae/blog/employee-training-importance/
3. https://www.mdx.ac.uk/our-research/centres/work-and-learning-research-centre
4. https://hbr.org/2016/07/a-global-survey-on-the-ambiguous-state-of-employee-trust
5. https://www.thebalance.com/incentives-and-benefits-for-greater-employee-engagement-4003007

6. MYTH #6

1. http://www.incentivefederation.org/wp-content/uploads/2016/07/Incentive-Marketplace-Estimate-Research-Study-2015-16-White-Paper.pdf

ENDNOTES

WHICH ENGAGEMENT PROGRAM WILL YOU INTEGRATE TODAY?

1. https://www.cogzrewards.com/